THE EFFECTS OF STRESS ON ADDICTION

A CONSUMER ENGAGEMENT APPROACH HANDBOOK

STEPHEN N. ALAPBE M.A., PSY.D.

MINDSTIR MEDIA

Published by Mindstir Media, LLC
45 Lafayette Rd | Suite 181| North Hampton, NH 03862 | USA
1.800.767.0531 | www.mindstirmedia.com

Printed in the United States of America
ISBN-13: 978-1-961532-48-9

This book is dedicated to the Almighty God,
the giver of all knowledge and wisdom.

Great thanks to my wife, Lenu and children:
Sirayira, Barikome & Barieba for their support and
encouragement during the academic journey.

CONTENTS

INTRODUCTION

This book, **The Effect of Stress on Addiction: A Consumer Engagement Approach,** is one of the books of the current dispensation with the task to address issues of addiction, impacts, solutions, strategies, and the best approach to combat addiction. We are in an era of the effect of stress on addiction.

The effect of stress on addiction is simply the impact of stress on addiction. Many people might confuse the effect of stress of addiction concerning only people who are victims of addiction. To my clear understanding, the effect of stress on addiction is general to every person because of the current trends in the nation and the world. The Covid-19 pandemic and the challenges we face daily, including but not limited to working, various engagements, drugs and technology addictions, business activities, and other activities of our choice, have led us to have addiction from stress in one way or the other. We are in the crisis of the effect of stress on addiction together, and even the author is not left out.

The prevalence of addiction is a cause for concern in America. Findings (e.g., Goings, Hidalgo & McGovern, 2017) reveal the endemic nature of addiction among the diverse ethnic and multiracial groups in America is underestimated and under-investigated. Stress is a disease of the soul, body, and mind (Biswas-Diner, 2013). The effect of stress on addiction affects families, individuals, communities, and even the social and economic fabric of the nation (Van Worner & Davis, 2016). The discovery of technology (e.g., . the Internet) has added the toll of addiction manifesting as Facebook, Smartphones, Google, Twitter, etc., which are controlling the daily lives of most Americans (Zivnuska, Carlson, Harris & Harris, 2019)

The challenges of stress on addiction are enormous. Several questions were raised on how to engage clients victimized by addiction, principally drug and technology addictions and "burnt out" from job activities. Though several evidence-based approaches have been suggested and implemented, care providers and clinicians may lose sight of the fundamentals of client engagement. After many years of service as a direct care worker, psychiatric technician and therapist, behavior support professional, case worker, and clinician, The author discovered the tools that deliver excellent care services to our clients' matters. A holistic and comprehensive approach coupled with an active treatment care approach is needed to get the best results for our clients'. This book seeks to inform care providers, healthcare professionals, active participants in healthcare delivery, and role players how to improve on the existing standards and move forward. The academic performance of adolescents, college students, and other adults, could be enhanced by applying the principles highlighted in the book.

The various roles as a clinical psychologist, gerontologist, and certified behavior analyst with several years of academic qualifications and credentials equipped the author to grasp the intricacies of the subject matter. The author's research on "The Impact of Stress on Addiction" discovered from research stress caused by addiction encapsulates everybody, society, and not what the general population myopically referred to as the victims of addiction (Doba, 2013). Stress can trigger addictions manifesting itself in every area of our lives; for example, our eating habits, if excessive, may lead to an addiction. I have seen and assisted clients affected by psychiatric illness and psychological disorders of addiction, including depression, sexual disorders, anxiety, schizophrenia, bipolar, suicidal behaviors, paranoid, delusional, and co-occurring disorders in clinics, group homes, and hospitals. What inferred, the effect of stress on addiction is becoming an integral precursor of many psychiatric illnesses and psychological disorders. Care providers and healthcare professionals may have overlooked implementing appropriate client engagement strategies to get better options. The fault of these professionals is not deliberate but sometimes pressures from the delivery of treatment services. Since our clients are diverse, appropriate client engagement strategies are needed to get to the root of the problem.

To address the critical aspects of the client engagement approach, the author devoted a chapter to highlight some of the formidable elements. Only some parts may be effective, but harnessing and integrating other strategies can make a difference. This book is a must-read for healthcare professionals; in fact, all professionals will be able to reap the benefits of this book. It serves as a reminder and a ready tool for delivering excellent care services to clients. If you want to implement the best evidence technique for therapy, you have to apply the best client engagement approach to get the desired result. Treating clients suffering from stress-induced addiction must go hand in hand with better client engagement strategies. Clinicians and care providers aware of essential elements of the client engagement approach can apply the best evidence-based techniques appropriately.

The author has scenarios as a direct care provider and mental/behavioral technician where clients with psychological disorders scare healthcare workers in the behavioral unit during night shifts.

After reading notes about psychiatric illness, some care providers were scared of delivering care, primarily due to the perceived violent behaviors of the clients. The author has always opened themselves to be of assistance in these situations. They have always greeted the clients with a smile, offered snacks, and inquired if they were comfortable with their current food supply. After attending to their immediate basic needs, they requested to do their vital signs, and they complied. One of the remarks from the clients appalled the author: "You are a good man." The author relayed to the staffers on the unit and volunteered to attend to the direct care needs of clients with diverse psychiatric illnesses during an emergency. Unsurprisingly, they were voted the "most compassionate staff" during evaluation by the hospital management. This love and compassion for clients have become the cornerstone of treating them with dignity and respect in any assigned role of providing excellent care services to clients.

Love and passion can propels direct care worker to make a difference in client's lives. Positive emotion with smiling, being empathetic, treating clients with dignity and respect coupled with compassion equips me as a better care provider. As a former mental health technician in one of the behavioral health centers in America, establishment of excellent rapport, therapeutic relationship and therapeutic communication with clients produced better care giver's result. The author implemented most of the principles and elements mentioned in the book especially CBT and Positive Psychology vis-a-vis client engagement strategies. The author resolved altercations with clients in the unit and serve as a better role model in the delivery of excellent care services. You cannot make a positive impact and difference in client's lives if you lost sight of compassion, empathy, dignity and respect. Positive emotion matters! Love and passion for clients and job matters! Treating all clients whole-heartedly without discrimination matters! Readers of the book should remember we are all involved in diverse roles in the delivery of excellent care services together. We are all involved in the challenges of addiction because what happens to our neighbor matters (Doba, 2014)!

.A clarion call for everyone including clinicians, social workers, nurses, mental professionals, adults, and students to read the book and apply information given for better usage and applications. The issues of stress on addiction are dynamic including client engagement strategies. The author promised that the book is worth every Dollar spent on purchasing it. Happy readers be blessed reading the book.

PART I

THE EFFECT OF STRESS ON ADDICTION

The impact of stress on addiction is becoming a shared life experience in the United States (US). The effect of stress on addiction is an integral part of human activities in the American society. The access to illegal drugs and non-prescribed use of Opioids is likely to be an ongoing public health crisis in America (Hooten, et al. 2017). Recently, the CDC (Center for Disease Control) has declared opioids as one of the subtypes of heroin addiction as an epidemic affecting the lives of American youths and adults. Furthermore, the impact of stress from technology addiction could exacerbate addictive behaviors and endanger the lives of humans and their environment. In addition, modem society's use of the internet for networking, information, and globalization has adversely affected human health (Ron, Yang, & Liu, 2017).

The consequence of stress on addiction (e.g. internet, social media &Facebook) has contributed to the development of depression and mental health dysfunctions (Boomvisuchi &Kuladee, 2017; Brailovskala & Margraf, 2017). The occurrence of chronic traumatic stress on addiction could affect the normal brain/mental functioning leading to the onset of psychological disorders (Ousdal, et al. 2017). In their research, Pitman and authors (2012) have revealed neural adaptation to severe traumatic stress on addiction but failed to understand the consequences of traumatic stress on decision-making and capability for optimal choice behavior. Evidence profoundly linked various psychiatric disorders connected with chronic traumatic stress to addiction as a factor in poor decision-making (Calla, et al. 2010; Sebold, et al., 2014). This evidence supports that traumatic stress's impact on addiction could make people susceptible to psychiatric illness, negatively affecting decision-making (Huys, et al. 2015). Because of the detail, the author used a theoretical study completing a systematic review of the literature in analyzing and researching the issues affected by the impact of stress on addiction and examining solutions.

The impact of stress on addiction may cause suicide, including suicidal ideation and suicidal behaviors. Suicide is a trans-diagnostic mental health problem with serious public health consequences. Initially, biologically based studies on dispositions were associated with suicidality exhibited by family, twin, and adoption studies (Brent & Melhon, 2008), accompanied by heritability for suicidal ideation and behavior. Recent studies have discovered two vital biobehavioral constructs of threat sensitivity and inhibitory control (Rozak & Cuthbert, 2016; Nelson, et al... 2016) that directly connect to suicidal behavior. Individuals suffering from the impact of stress on addiction were prone to depression, suicidal ideation, suicidal behavior, and eventual death from suicide because of stressor, strain, and stress reactivity from the ailment (Venables, et al., 2018).

Doba (2014) considered anorexia nervosa and drug dependence disorder addictive behaviors because of stress on addiction. It found that drug dependence disorder and anorexia nervosa are addictions sharing some similarities based on psychology and pathology.

Addictive behavior is a process whereby a behavior occurs in an uncontrollable pattern and continues to escalate despite dire consequences. Many people suffering from the impact of stress on addiction continue to have ambivalence even after a relapse. They might continue to engage in the habit after treatment and recovery. The stress from addiction borne by families, communities, states, and the country is an illness not just of the individual but also of the whole family. Any change in the behavior of an individual suffering from addictive stress could ultimately affect the family system and degenerate into the communities. The entire family could be associated with strain, stressor, and stressor reactivity that emanated from working with patients suffering from addiction, such as alcohol intoxication, drug abuse, substance abuse, and substance use disorders. The adverse effects were viral-like epidemic. The impact of stress on addiction is a precursor to major stress-related diseases (e.g., depression) that reverberate through the family system and interactions with members of society. The economic cost of the treatment for patients suffering from various addictions in the country runs into billions of dollars (Van Wormer & Davis, 2016). Addiction was erratic and destructive in operation. A family's psychological and social well-being is devastated by stress in the context of addiction (Van Wormer & Davis, 2016).

Stress from addictive behaviors could cause job strain, a significant problem-affecting people working in the labor force connected with job burnout, psychological fatigue, and chronic ailments. A landmark study successfully assessed the level of job strain among civilians in the workforce and evaluated the consequence of job strain on job burnout, psychological fatigue, and chronic diseases (Guan et al., 2017). A representative sample made up of 300 civil servants was investigated in a cross-sectional study from the period of March to August 2014. Measuring scales and tools consisting of the Personal Strain Questionnaire (PSQ), Maslach Burnout Inventory (MBI), and Multidimensional Fatigue Inventory (MFI-20) were used respectively as a structured method to assess job for strain level, job burnout, and mental fatigue. The results revealed 33.8% of the civilian labor force was suffering from a high and moderate level of job strain. The breakdown from the characteristics with a higher-job strain level indicated that the following factors assessed with such stress being female from Uygur, a Turkish ethnic group with lower educational attainment level and job title rank, a shorter period of working experience, workers with marriage status, and those at the lower-income level. Workers who suffered from chronic ailments were mainly susceptible to hypertension and coronary heart disease amounted to 18.5%. At the same time, those with a high-job strain level showed enhanced rates of burnout, mental fatigue scores, and experience with chronic diseases. A multiple linear regression model made up of three indicator variables in job burnout amounted to 45.0% of its occurrence, which included the following: female gender, lower-wage level, and elevated job strain in workers. The susceptibility to chronic dysfunction was more significant in workers with high job burnout and psychological fatigue scores compared to workers with lower scores. The data collated from the study portray evidence for the impacts of job strain connected with job bum out, psychological fatigue, and chronic ailments among the civilian labor force (Guan, et al., 2017).

The effect of stress on addiction manifested in different areas affects clients' lives. Another consequence was sleep disturbance and other related effects. Chen and colleagues (2017) conducted a cross-sectional descriptive study on sleep disturbance and its connections with the severity of stress on addiction, dependence, depression, and quality of life among individuals who have abused heroin. Previous research studies relied solely on patients getting treatment. The present research examines the I-month prevalence of sleep disturbance of stress on addiction and its connections with socio-demographic substance-related features, severe effects of dependence, depression, and quality of life among heroin-dependent patients before the treatment program. The result revealed that consumers who depended on heroin experienced an I-month severe sleep disturbance effect linked with chronic dependence severity, increased incidence of depression, and lower physical health dysfunction affecting the quality of life. Sleep disturbance was one of the common effects of stress on addiction that affected the lives of consumers suffering from heroin addiction and negatively impacted treatment outcomes, mental health dysfunctions, and quality of life (Chen, et al., 2017).

Currently, the effect of stress on internet addiction is a primary concern affecting the lives of students. The impact was felt in the general population because internet usage was accessible. The addictive behavior is described as uncontrollable internet use negatively affecting daily life routines, relationships, and emotional balance. It is a growing issue in today's society characterized by excessive use, withdrawal, intolerance, and negative consequences. Boonvisuchi and Kuladee (2017) found that more than 50% of people with Internet addiction (IA) have severe dysfunction in academic, relationship, financial and occupational stress-related problems. In Asia, the occurrence of IA varies from 1% to 36.7% based on various assessment tools and study populations.

Disproportionately, college students have a higher incidence of IA than the general population and adolescents. IA is considered a common psychological problem among Thai medical students, and the study also revealed depression and academic problems connected with IA.

The impact of stress on addiction has negatively affected the health of consumers, families, communities, and society. Stress can affect recovery from addiction disorders. The statistics of deaths from drug overdose have risen significantly in the United States. It reported that since 2000, there had been a 137 percent rise in the rate of deaths caused by drug overdose, including a 200 percent spike in the rate of drug overdose deaths due to opioids (i.e., opioid pain relievers and heroin). From 2014, 47,055 drug overdose deaths occurred in the US, with a breakdown showing a 1-year rise of 6.5 percent. The incidence of drug overdose deaths skyrocketed for both sexes, ranging between ages 25-44 years and greater than or equal to 55 years, non-Hispanic Whites and non-Hispanic Blacks, in the Northeastern, Midwestern, and Southern regions of the United States. The rate of deaths from opioid overdose rose significantly from 7.9 per 100,000 in 2013 to 9.0 per 100,000 in 2014, representing a 14 percent increase overall (www.cdc.gov).

Doba (2014) highlighted the negative impact of stress on addiction and described it as a monster affecting the psychological and social well-being of families and society. The jet age of technology has exacerbated the stress connected with internet addiction, causing social anxiety and other related concerns (Chen, et al. 2017, Ren, Yang & Liu, 2017). The stress impact on addiction has various adverse effects on individuals and the social environment. It is a vehicle that makes individuals overwork, overeats, overdrink, etc., which later becomes an addiction. In essence, it diminishes interpersonal relationships while accelerating deterioration related to aging prematurely and brain health. The stress symptoms from addiction are responsible for causing psychological, physiological, and psychiatric illnesses in the body. There are physical, social, and psychological manifestations of addiction and related stress in our lives; Stressors from addiction occur in the mind and body and negatively affect our physical and emotional entitlements. Other psychological and physiological symptoms of stress from addiction include anxiety, depression, phobias, binge eating, diarrhea, constipation, hypertension, insomnia, substance and drug abuse, and suicidal behaviors, among other negative experiences. (Block, Block & Porters, 2012).

Negative Effects of Stress on Addiction

The continuous stress from addiction could have long-term adverse effects on victims' psychological health and social well-being throughout their life span (DiLillo, 2001; Ogle, Rubin, & Sieger, 2013). Despite experiencing interpersonal trauma, clients might confront impairments in physical and spiritual health that degenerate into cognitive growth and disengagement in their career prospects (Banks, 2006; Perez, Abrams, Lopez-Martinez, & Asmundson, 2012). Moreover, individuals who experienced interpersonal trauma from the stress of an addiction might undergo a sense of betrayal, powerlessness, hopelessness, and stigmatization (Williams, RIFE, & Cantrell, 2015; Platt & Freyd, 2015), which could contribute to distorted self-concept and worldview. Cognitive behavioral therapy (CBT) and Positive Psychology principles (e.g. positive emotions) can restore the psychological health and well-being of affected addictive stress clients.

The negative effect of stress on addiction is felt in time distortion when users at-risk for social media addiction engage in non-social media tasks (Turel, Brewers & Bechara, 2018). Individuals who are addicted to the use of social media such as Facebook, Snapchat, and Twitter are regarded as a unique form of technology addiction yet has similarity in symptomatology with "Internet gaming disorder," which is now under Section 3 of the DSM-5 (American Psychiatric Association, 2013). Social media addiction is a state of uncontrollable exposure and engagement in the addictive use of social media platforms, including excessive time and effort that may negatively affect other important life matters (Dong & Potenza, 2014), and relapse (Andreassen, 2016). Evidence abounds showed behavioral and neuro-psychological factors for stress and addiction-related symptoms that negatively affect people with more profound addictions (Banyai, et al; 2017, Dong, et al, 2012). Information about social media addiction is obtained through self-reporting and clinical interviews (Andreassen, et al, 2016). Current studies have indicated the need for objective markers for such addictions that support surveys and clinical interviews. This was necessary because self-reports might be biased in core symptoms that use time estimates, compulsion, overuse and tolerance (Lin, et al, 2015; Rau, et al, 2008). Such research revealed that these concerns were in line with time perception theories (Takahashi, et al, 2008; Wilson, et al, 2015; Witnam & Paulus, 2008) as time distortion can be used as an indicator in the classification of individuals to addiction versus non-addictive groups. A combination of Positive Psychology and CBT was helpful in reducing the harmful effects of stress on drugs and technology addictions.

EFFECT OF STRESS ON DRUG ADDICTION

· · · · ·

The access to illegal drugs and non-prescribed use of Opioids is likely to be an ongoing public health crisis in America (Hooten, et al., 2017). Drug addiction is defined as a strong urge or impulse compulsion to use a substance, an enhanced tolerance to the substance, both physiological and psychological dependence on the substance, and being knowledgeable of dire consequences of social, physical problems or psychological problems based on (DSM-IV) worldwide definition of classification of mental disorders. Researchers have not come up with a unanimous decision about the causes of the impact of stress on addiction (Koski-Jannes, et al., 1998).

Many causes have been postulated for opiate addiction. Genetic explanations stress family pedigree as a leading cause (Hyytia, 2003). Neurobiological theories state a description of the development of addiction based on positive, enjoyable, and negative, undesirable reinforcement of brain roles (2005). Rational theories suggest dependence as a reliable choice to deal with particular problems of drugs for self-medication motives. Psychodynamic theories clarify addiction as a negative personality development revealed through issues of self-gratification, incapability of self-growth, and object relations problems (Granstru & Kaoppasalmi, 2003). Most of the dominant contributions acknowledged the impact of stress on addiction as being located within the body or brain of a person while describing alcohol dependence as problematic and treated as a symptom of a unique primary inner disorder (Keanne, 2002).

The dominant worldview of addiction failed to understand the fluidity and the depressive effects of alcohol consumption patterns in their explanations (Dilkes-Frayne, et al., 2017). Despite the popular opinion used in explaining the impact of stress on addiction, it is conceptualized by pinpointing social or cultural areas as one of the primary factors considered in the explanation. An example is drawn from Hanninen and Koski-Jennes (1999), who uses narrative analysis to autobiographies in explaining the impact of stress on addiction to drinking, different types of drug use, binge eating, smoking, gambling, and sex indulgence.

EFFECT OF STRESS ON TOBACCO ADDICTION

• • • • •

Another psychological factor that affected the impact of stress on addiction was tobacco addiction. Several investigations going on disorders of addiction based on public perception concentrated much on alcohol and illegal drugs instead of behaviors of addiction. A study evaluated general addictive behaviors, including pornography, gambling, alcohol, and substances like marijuana and heroin. There are negative public perceptions and stigmatization of people with alcohol intoxication and substance abuse disorders. One can easily detect stigmatization by asking participants about the desire to associate with people with uncommon psychiatric disorders and conditions of addiction (Lang & Rosenberg, 2017).

Public perceptions of drug abuse are assessed by inquiring how people define drug addiction. Using the Diagnostic and Statistical Manual of Mental Disorders for substance use disorder, two subscales that showed "appetitive" and "compulsive" areas of addiction were used. The appetitive subscale comprises behaviors that share a willingness to smoke and continue tobacco use despite dire consequences. The compulsive subscale indicated aspects of impaired control and psychological/physiological dependence. As a result, the researchers in the present study applied a between-subjects design to evaluate ordinary people's perceptions of individuals categorized as being addicted to either pornography or gambling, alcohol, marijuana, or heroin (Lang & Rosenberg, 2017).

Pathological gambling was chosen as one of the two behavioral addictions since the Diagnostic and Statistical Manual-Fifth Edition (DSM-5) classified it as an addictive disorder with attributes of preoccupation with gambling, the likelihood of losing a job or close relationships, and a penchant to borrow money from other people. Pornography was chosen because hyperactive sexuality includes uncontrollable use of pornography and has characteristics such as cravings, tolerance, impaired control, and negative results associated with substance use disorders (APA, 2013). The results reveal that public perception was more robust against the willingness to associate with the person with any addiction (Lang & Rosenberg, 2017).

Genetically, similar factors led to a high incidence of alcohol and tobacco comorbidity and dependence. This was because the two were commonly used together. Several factors have been identified; prominent among them were psychosocial, environmental, and biological factors responsible for a high incidence of comorbidity and dependence based on evidence that supported their different roles and the association between them (Otto, et al., 2017).

Behavioral genetic studies could give knowledge about the roles of environmental and heritable factors responsible for environmental, psychosocial, and biological characteristics. Different percentages accounted for shared and specific environmental factors as well as exposure to alcohol dependence based on gender and ethnicity. Forty-eight percent was linked to variation to liability to alcohol dependence caused by heritable factors, thus portraying the similar etiology and chemistry' occurrence between environmental factors and genetic factors associated with alcohol and tobacco use and ad-diction (Otto, et al., 2017).

The investigation deduced multiple biological pathways that acted on the analyses. This pathway categorizes different variants across different genes, which increase our knowledge of the chemis-try involved in alcohol and tobacco use and dependence. The results showed variants with these genes responsible for widespread expo-sure to psychopathology rather than specific substance risk factors (Otto, et al., 2017).

Adolescents living in a substance abuse center were more vul-nerable to tobacco use than the general population. The substance abuse treatment failed to be a correction program for predisposed victims—a study undertaken to assess tobacco use and psychiatric comorbidity among adolescents in a treatment facility. Cigarette smoking from tobacco use has a higher incidence of deaths com-pared to other adolescents exposed to smoking in a treatment center (e.g., substance abuse) than in the general population. The critical period for inhaling tobacco starts in the adolescent developmental years which continues to escalate until adulthood. The penchant for nicotine dependence continues to grow with risk factors of anxiety disorder, alcohol intoxication, and other disorders associated with substance abuse (Cole et al., 2012).

Substance users in the population considered smoking tobacco, which translated to substance abuse treatment centers. As a result, there was a decrease in post-treatment of alcohol and chug use com-pared to the high incidence of cigarette smoking among adolescents in substance abuse. It discovered that adults and adolescents have comorbid psychiatric behavioral addictions that include mood dis-orders and conduct disorders prone to high risk of cigarette con-sumption. Other researchers also found that affective disorders, drug abuse, and dependence were more closely linked with nicotine dependence than tobacco use. In early adulthood, habitual smokers were more predisposed to alcohol and drug dependence, including depression and anxiety disorders (Cole et al., 2012).

The craving for tobacco use is the primary motivator for smoking addictive behavior. Craving was one of the criteria for tobacco dependence based on the Diagnostic and Statistical Manual of Mental Disorders fifth edition (DSM-5) (APA, 2013). Indeed, it is a cardinal factor in addiction. Cravings are an urge or desire to inhale tobacco measured by self-report. It is differentiated into two types in the form of regular, daily inhalers of tobacco. The first was a general craving based on thought, which can be slow and linked to previous smoking. Cue-specific craving takes place when a regular drug user is exposed to a drug-related cue, which can increase or raise the need for smoking (Gass & Tiffany, 2017).

Cue-specific craving was demonstrated in the laboratory using experimental control to regulate the general level of investigations. The relationship between craving and smoking was investigated under laboratory conditions using different behaviors that positively showed smoking behavior. Measurement based on index consumption and assessment seeking is used in determining behavioral outcomes. Consumption measures the traits of how people inhale tobacco, and the number of cigarettes smoked in fixed intervals. Assessment seeking tobacco implies all behavior is undertaken that results in inhaling a cigar. Three tobacco use behaviors of consumption, non-automatic seeking, and automatic seeking as a paradigm are used in the assessment in development and initial validation of the current study (Gass & Tiffany, 2017).

Tobacco use or nicotine use is considered a form of behavioral addiction. There has been a rising tide in the consumption of cigarettes all over the world. Addiction was not a single phenomenon, but it integrated several characteristics, including repetitive involvement in behaviors that reward, loss of control, continuous use of an addictive substance despite dire consequences, and withdrawal symptoms due to physical dependence. Behavioral "addictions" have the same traits as substance addiction, which possess features of maladaptive and repetitive behaviors. This approach to addiction leads to the recognition of ' Substance-Related and Addictive Disorders,' including gambling disorder as classified by the Diagnostic and Statistical Manual of Mental Disorders (5thed) (DSM-5) (APA, 2013). The term "addiction" originated from psychoactive substances that include cocaine, alcohol, or nicotine substances with addictive characteristics that have similar effects on the brain's reward pathways, especially the ventral striatum (Chamberlain et al., 2016).

Substance disorder clients discovered susceptibility to the use of tobacco products. The rate of tobacco consumption among people with substance abuse disorders was very high in America and other developed countries of the world (Tywyman, Bonesvki, Paul & Bryant, 2018). The occurrence of tobacco smoking is inversely related to socioeconomic status (SES) in high-income and advanced countries of the world. For instance, in the case of Australia, the occurrence of smoking people in the lowest SES was 24.6 percent compared to 12.5 percent with individuals in the high SES zones. Peak rates of smoking found among a group of people coupled with low SES have other distinguishing attributes from the general population that included indigenous groups (31-51.8 %), people with a mental malfunction (31.7-32.4%), individuals with substance abuse disorders (77%), homeless (73%), and incarcerated people (78-84%) (Tywyman, Bonesvki, Paul & Bryant, 2018).

Individuals suffering from substance abuse disorder who were exposed to smoking at an early age would likely become habitual smokers or develop nicotine dependence. They might become 'die-hard smokers' with difficulty leaving smoking (Shu & Cook, 2015). The use of tobacco products can be prolonged consumption as tobacco addicts find it difficult to quit smoking. The habit of using tobacco products might degenerate into tobacco addiction.

Impulsiveness is a personality trait found among people with addictions. Impulsiveness is the susceptibility to a sudden, unexpected reaction to internal and external stimuli despite dire consequences. The term applied as a multidimensional construct in which the behavior involved in the act was unstoppable with cognitive impairments. The individual committing the behavior cannot discern the consequences of destructive behaviors. The result led to chronic smoking, alcohol addiction, and pathological gambling. Impulsiveness was a risk factor in alcohol addiction and other types of addictions. It might play dual roles in both psychoactive substance and behavioral addictions as an essential determining factor for the growth of addiction and as a consequence. Smoking tobacco products and alcohol consumption are described as a desire for reward or momentary gratification (Bodor, et al., 2015).

The problem of addictions was causing concern for clinicians, healthcare providers, and the government. The need for better treatment and prevention were critical issues confronting society. There was a need to apply a holistic, comprehensive approach to treat tobacco use disorder because of its comorbidity with other disorders. Tobacco use disorder has comorbidity with several disorders, such as substance abuse disorder, ADHD, conduct disorder, depressive disorder, anxiety disorders, personality disorders, and psychiatric disorders. Evidence showed patients in early-stage recovery from other drugs or alcohol tend to smoke or chew tobacco at a high level (APA, 2013).

One of the methods for preventing tobacco and drug addictions was behavioral pharmacology. The U.S. Food and Drug Administration depended on this principle to curtail and regulate tobacco products and drugs. It was used as a scientific discipline that incorporated the principle of careful empirical assessment of the relationship between drugs and respecting individual organisms. Reliability and validity are used scientifically in behavioral pharmacology to obtain better results. The FDA regulated tobacco and drugs' effects on the central nervous system by combating the abuse and neglect by pharmaceutical companies and tobacco product manufacturers (Henningfield, Buchalter, & Fant, 2016).

The excessive smoking of tobacco products and drugs and illegal consumption of substances have profound effects in increasing malfunctions in the psychological and social lives of victims and neurobiological dysfunctions in addicts. Nicotine can directly or indirectly raise dopamine levels in the neural 'reward system.' It might influence the production of solid reinforcement effects. The continuous use of nicotine is linked with changes in neurotransmitter systems. Prominent reactions in the latter led to a decrease in dopamine receptors and dopamine transporter available in the striatum, affecting dopamine levels negatively (Chamberlain; et al., 2016).

Treating tobacco addiction and other comorbid disorders is effective in therapy where medications are combined with behavioral therapies. Better medications are found to be effective for treating nicotine dependence, drug addictions, and behavioral addictions, especially those that deal with the glutamatergic activity. Glutamate helps treat impulsivity, craving, attentional problems, and relapse. One of the prominent medications found effective is N-acetyl cysteine. This amino acid brings back extracellular glutamate levels in the nucleus acumens, decreasing reward-seeking behavior in consumers with various substance addictions, including tobacco and marijuana cravings. Memantine, a pharmacological agent having glutamatergic effects, has been found effective in treating behavioral addictions and substance use disorders. The use of memantine is a medication used to reduce the primary influence of cigarette smoking and heroin used inside the vein (Chamberlain et al., 2016).

Smoking has become an endemic disease in the U.S. despite dire consequences. However, evidence of a decline in smoking, the number of people quitting smoking was still abysmal low in percentage (5%). Several factors are affecting the relapse rate. This might involve stress, adverse effects, and depression. There was a need to take the necessary steps to prevent relapse and increase the cessation rate. Many methods have been recommended for preventing relapse and cessation rates. One of the breakthrough interventions was applying mindfulness-based treatments specifically for nicotine dependence and substance abuse disorders. Mindfulness is a form of meditation by paying close attention to what is happening now, being nonjudgmental, and directing more attention to the present while experiencing moment-to-moment awareness. A principal aspect of mindfulness is disregarding all emotions, negative thinking, perceptions, and sensations as mere thinking. These will go a long way in a moment while focusing on the present. Practicing mindfulness will make a difference and affect the lives of smokers undergoing smoking cessation and relapse (Vidrine et al., 2016).

Mindfulness practice is a panacea for tobacco smokers and individuals suffering from drug and substance addictions, including behavioral addictions. The clinicians' duty was to train consumers in the proper application of mindfulness training. This practice occurred in a serene environment where consumers should be in the mood for meditation. Clients are placed in a quiet room where they can lie on the ground or sit comfortably in a chair where instruction is given. Clients should remain focused on the present and regard negative thoughts as mere thinking. The awareness that these thoughts will go away and concentrate on the present. Doing this will uplift your inner self and give you the strength and ability to tackle stressful situations (Vidrine et al., 2016).

There were two evidence-based treatments for smoking cessation and relapse, which have stood the test of time. The two widely used treatments are mindfulness-based stress reduction (MBSR) and mindfulness-based cognitive therapy (MBCT). The former is primarily used for patients suffering from stress and pain-related disorders, while the latter is introduced to deal with consumers suffering from chronic or recurrent depressive disorders. Meditation was the focal point of teaching mindfulness applied for the two interventions. MBSR, when used in different settings, has a successful intervention, especially when patients are in anxious and depressive mood states. MBCT has proven effective in preventing relapse to depression for people suffering from nicotine dependence and substance use disorders (Vidrine et al., 2016).

Mindfulness-based therapies have been found effective for treating patients suffering from nicotine dependence. When consumers used mindfulness meditation, the result showed a drastic reduction in stress and psychological distress. It showed a reduction in smoking urges, a rise in acceptance and awareness, and a decrease in cravings. Because of its simple application, mindfulness practice can take place in any room with a reduced noise level, and no distraction as the participant systematically applies the steps for the meditation (Vidrine et al., 2016).

A special type of mindfulness-based treatment earmarked for smoking is mindfulness-based addiction treatment (MBAT). This was introduced as a new behavioral treatment to address the problem of failed attempts to stop smoking, rise in the levels of nicotine dependence, and other comorbid disorders. Mindfulness-based therapies have broad applications in decreasing psychological distress across different spectrums of the population and conditions. It is effective in smoking cessation, recovery of smoking lapse, and other essential improvements in comorbid tobacco disorders (Vidrine et al., 2016).

The current research used an expanded clinical randomized trial to assess a mindfulness-based treatment for nicotine dependence or substance abuse disorder. Results showed that MBAT effectively enhanced recovery from lapse smoking cessation and abstinence post-treatment. Mindfulness could play a prominent role in the study in preventing relapse and negative cognitions when mindfulness is integrated with smoking cessation, the result outstanding lowering the effects of lapse and encouraging recovery from abstinence. If mindfulness is applied correctly, die-hard smokers can make a difference in the improvement of smoking cessation and reduced relapse. Hence, MBAT is a relapse-prevention intervention strategy to combat smoking cessation, nicotine dependence, and relapse, even in alcohol treatment (Vidrine et al., 2016). More research is needed to substantiate the effectiveness of MBAT as a breakthrough intervention in addiction.

EFFECT OF STRESS ON TECHNOLOGY ADDICTION

• • • • •

Internet addiction operates in various forms (e.g., Facebook, Google, Twitter & Smartphone). One of the recent ones was "smartphone addiction" (Barashdi, Bouazza, & Jabur, 2015). Smartphone users cover different age groups, from adolescents to young adults. The discovery of new technology has boosted economic activities and world inventions. College students were among the most vulnerable and targeted cohorts for the new invention. Advertisers for the consumption of smartphones have chosen college students as their largest consumers and large markets (Head & Ziolowski, 2012). Despite the advantages accruing from the use of smartphones, there is the other side of the coin, as problems emanating from the use of smartphones are found in the population (Ahmed, Ramzed, & Qazi, 2011).

Smartphone use is becoming indispensable for students because of its various applications: the enjoyment of games and face-to-face communication benefits regular cellphone use. The use of the mobile phone to surf the internet and escape unpleasant situations continues to make dependence on smartphones unsurmountable (Casey, 2012). It argued that smartphone addiction is mainly found among college students because of the accessibility to uncontrollable and continuous use of cell phones (Bianchi & Phillips, 2005). Researchers have discovered evidence of behavioral obsession among university students who engage in the excessive use of smartphones (Walsh, White, & Young, 2008).

Behavioral addiction criteria based on symptoms include behavioral, cognitive balance, conflict with other challenging activities, euphoria, tolerance, withdrawal, relapse, and reinstatement found at different levels among college students who frequent cell phone users. Other researchers like Hassan, Zadeh, and Rezael (2011) described text-message dependency as text messaging-linked compulsive behavior responsible for psychological or behavioral symptoms with negative social consequences. The investigations revealed that college students are victims of the impact of stress on smartphone addiction. This might become a significant health problem among university students. Physiologically, psychological distress can be associated with maladaptive Internet and smartphone use (Devis-Devis et al., 2009).

The impact of stress on addiction has comorbidities due to adverse effects on consumers. Online gaming addiction has comorbidity with substance dependence and pathological gambling (Kuss & Griffiths, 2012). Online gaming has become a continuous, excessive habit for children and adolescents. The latest report from the Entertainment Software Association (ESA) stated that 25 percent of computer and video game players constituted those under the age of 18 years, and 60 percent are male. The ESA also revealed that 25 percent of parents did not restrict the time limit for children's use of the internet and the period for video and computer games (ESA, 2010).

Researchers have identified online gaming addiction in extreme conditions associated with substance dependence with the characteristics of salience, mood modification, craving, and intolerance (Hsu, Wen, & WII, 2009; Ko et al., 2009; Mehroof & Griffiths, 2010; Wolfling, Grisser, & Thalamann, 2008; Young, 2009). Recently, criteria developed for the diagnosis of online gaming addiction in empirical studies have been associated with the criteria for pathological gambling or substance dependence. Pathological gambling is characterized by consistent and recurrent maladaptive gambling activities displayed by five or more symptoms: preoccupation with gambling, continuous desire to gamble with an excessive amount of money to get expected excitement, and uncontrollable or restless attempts to reduce or stop gambling. Gambling is a means of escape from problems or to relieve stress; a penchant for gambling despite losing an excessive amount of money and pathological lying to family members and significant others to continue gambling. In addition, committed crimes for forgery, fraud, thief, or embezzlement caused by gambling, disruption or loss in a committed relationship because of gambling, and finally, the absence of manic episodes associated with pathological gambling. (APA, 2013).

The treatment for opioid dependence and comorbid posttraumatic stress disorder (PTSD) was a concern for clinicians. There was a lack of evidence-based practices for treating this comorbidity. It was cumbersome to separate the symptoms between PTSD and opiate dependence. Specifically, opioid withdrawal symptoms similarity to hypervigilance and escalated sudden response of patients with PTSD (Fareed et al., 2013). It was still unknown whether cannabis usage was a causal risk factor for the growth of schizophrenia-related psychosis associated with mania. Studies have also revealed that people diagnosed with bipolar disorder are associated with cannabis use and escalation of mania symptoms (Gibles et al., 2015).

The impact of stress on heroin addiction was a growing concern among the aging 'baby boomers' generation,' and the condition would continue to deteriorate (Han et al., 2009). Heroin addiction was second in rank to alcohol addiction as the primary substance of choice for adults over the age of 50 admitted for substance abuse treatment (Liftwall, Schuster, & Stain, 2006). The impact of stress on heroin addiction among older adults has health consequences for this population (Rosen et al., 2011). Due to aging, the elderly who are heroin addicts are susceptible to physical and physiological dysfunctions that affect their well-being and health conditions. Older adults that engage in heroin addiction are vulnerable to diabetes, heart problems, arthritis, and other psychiatric ailments because of complications of stress on addiction.

CHAPTER SUMMARY/ KEY TAKEAWAYS

The negative effects of stress on addiction have affected people in various ways.

- Psychological health and social well-being of addicted clients adversely affected.
- Interpersonal trauma effect degenerated to a sense of betrayal, powerlessness, hopelessness, and stigmatization with the concomitant distorted self-concept and worldview.
- CBT & PT, 2 empirically and evidence-based interventions highly recommended for therapy.
- Social media/ technology addiction has similarity with "Internet gaming disorder" recognized by DSM-5 (APA, 2013).
- Opioid crisis in America ongoing endemic.
- Stigmatization & negative perceptions of Tobacco addictive users.
- Alcohol & Tobacco addictions have comorbidity and dependence.
- Tobacco addiction may cause mood and conduct disorders, affective & anxiety disorders, drug abuse & substance use, ADHD, personality and psychiatric disorders.
- Behavioral Pharmacology & Mindfulness Practice (e.gs. MBSR, MBCT & MBAT) for recovery and relapse prevention, and combating smoking cessation, nicotine dependence and relapse even in alcohol treatment.

In the next chapter, readers will acquaint with client engagement approach strategies for the effect of stress on addiction. Clients suffering from addiction are facing herculean task of recovery and coping with negative impact of stress on addiction. The principles suggested are client-friendly with the ultimate goal of getting excellent treatment care for clients.

Client Engagement
Approach Strategies

P roviding treatment services to clients suffering from stress-caused addiction can be a frustrating experience. Mental health professionals with diverse roles as therapists, clinicians, counselors, and teachers confront a daunting task in treatment. The frustrating experience is growing, especially with clients with stress-caused addiction. In my daily assignments as a treatment specialist, clients might have an uncompromising attitude toward therapy. The client is ambivalent and refuses to answer simple, straightforward questions: can you reduce the number of cigarettes per day to half? Can you minimize beer consumption from six cans to three cans daily? Can I refer you to a tobacco cessation program? Can you join the Alcoholics Anonymous (AA) group? Many clients respond in divergent ways. Some might say: "I cannot join for now, but later in the future." Others might say blatantly, "I do not think tobacco cessation or alcohol cessation is my problem for now." (Dougherty-Hunt, 1988).

The impact of stress caused by various addictions, including opioids, tobacco, alcohol, and technology, are clearly in symptoms exhibited in moods, demeanor, and emotions. Applying the client engagement approach can positively impact clients' lives. Using the first step in AA, "We admitted we were powerless over all alcohol (addictions) – that our lives have become unimaginable (AA, 1953)". Experience has shown that using force or cohesion in therapy would fail. Appreciation, collaboration, and engagement in a face-to-face approach with clients as joint partners or co-pilots of the journey of tackling stress issues might be successful (Dougherty-Hunt, 1988).

The negative impact of stress on addiction is devastating to clients, and how to come out from it might be a mirage. Clinicians, therapists, counselors, and mental health professionals may apply faith-based and spirituality in intervening in issues of addiction staring in their faces. For care, providers of Christian faith using prayer to God can say: "God give us the grace to accept with serenity the things cannot be changed, courage to change the things which should be changed, and the wisdom to distinguish the one from the order" (Niebuhr, 1978).

I suggest the answer to the care provider's dilemma is client engagement strategies, discussed below. Flexibility in dealing with clients' problems, goals-oriented objectives, and evidence-based interventions is worthwhile for achieving the desired result in therapy. Client's challenges demand a change in approach on the part of clinicians when providing treatment to victims of addiction.

In mental health sciences, engagement implies the totality of efforts made during therapy, initially from intake sessions, to achieve the desired results. It is a multiple construct with several divisions, such as communication, participation, and exchange of essential information (Holdsworth, Bowen, & Howat, 2014). Specifically, in mental health, engagement is described as the strengths-based process of healing connection with mental clients and care providers that support their recovery in synergy with family, culture, and community. It is a goal-oriented interactive process for recovery for clients and mental health care providers. National Alliance on Mental Illness (NAMI), 2010) described engagement as a new standard for mental health care and practice. Engagement extended the concepts of person-centered care and the therapeutic relationship.

The client Engagement Approach (CEA) for victims of addiction is crucial for improving their emotional well-being and mental health. CEA should focus on growing both old and new clients. Practitioners should not focus only on new clients because the old clients' needs are forgotten, and their psychological needs worsen. This occurred during the COVID-19 pandemic when older adults with disability and victims of addiction and psychological disorders were neglected, increasing the suicide rate. This was highlighted in the Forbes (2020) article: "Leadership: The Power of a Client Engagement Strategy," where silence with clients suffering from addictive stress and various psychological disorders (e.g., depression) is described as a danger to business. The onus is on mental health professionals to provide excellent service to old clients and a better experience for new clients.

Research shows empathy is the most critical leadership quality embedded in compassion (Forbes, 2020). Compassion incorporates empathy as an essential strategy in delivering excellent care for clients with addictive stress. Healthcare providers should have the critical skill of demonstrated leadership in healthcare delivery services. Compassion and empathy work together to provide the best services to clients with addictive stress. Empathy, as it applies to business leaders, is also a dependable tool for all mental health professionals (Forbes, 2020).

PERSON-CENTERED PLANNING (PCP)

• • • • •

Person-Centered Planning (PCP) connects the client engagement approach to achieve the best result in delivering health care services. CEA vis-à-vis PCP is pursuing the same goal. CEA involves talking, speaking, interacting, and communicating with clients therapeutically, resulting in building a therapeutic relationship. PCP is discovering how a client wants to live a productive life and the requirements to actualize the dream (Ritchie et al., 2003).

Ritchie et al. (2003) pinpointed the objective of person-centered planning: "good planning leading to positive changes in people's lives and services." Clinicians, social workers, and mental health professionals have used different methods to achieve the overall target of affecting positive changes in clients' lives and services.

The growth of psychological and mental health services needed in America is alarming. The challenges may become unsurmountable if PCP & CEA neglect providing excellent treatment and social services to clients of addiction and other psychological disorders. By integrating CEA and PCP in therapy, the goal of providing excellent services to clients of addictive stress and psychological disorders is actualized. The main issue in PCP & CEA is client focus, and wishes must be paramount and upheld. The clinician's view should focus on the client and transcend other providers' views in the planning process.

MOTIVATIONAL INTERVIEWING (MI)

· · · · ·

Motivational Interviewing (MI) enhances the client engagement approach. MI has become a critical component of client CEA in delivering excellent treatment services to addictive stress people. CEA entails focusing and engaging in MI. When integrated, the MI and CEA assist clients in identifying and changing behaviors, enhancing optional life goals and mental health functioning. Care providers and clinicians must engage, talk, and ask evocative questions while looking for pros and cons with clients in therapy (Miller & Rollnick, 2002).

Since MI is a person-centered and goal-oriented system of communicating with clients, it should focus on motivating clients to change and resolving ambivalence arising during the engagement. Ambivalence is one of the critical ingredients of MI, as addictive clients might have double feelings when engaging in change talk. Addictive stress spiraled in mental health, co-occurring with depression, suicide, anxiety, and substance misuse (MaGPI Research Group, 2003).

MI is a collaborative, goal-oriented, and therapeutic approach developed to assist addictive clients (e.g., alcohol addiction) in changing their addictive behavior (Miller & Rollnick, 2002). The MI initiated by Miller and Rollnick is based on a technique to allow people to identify their problems and the readiness, ability, and willingness to change. It was a conversational person-focused system of communication whereby an ambivalent client undergoes a step-by-step process to change during the therapy session. The effects of MI on addictive stress clients would lead to reduced depression, reduced prescription misuse, enhanced self-efficacy, and enhanced motivation to change (Hanera, 2014).

Collaboratively, MI with empathy and CEA, acknowledging friendship with change, and enhancing self-efficacy with reinforcing discussions are cardinal for achieving the desired result. The systematic approach outlined in MI can change the perceptions of ambivalence by addictive stress clients at the end of the therapy session. With MI and CEA, an addictive client could present arguments for desired therapy changes. The responsibility for change lies with the addictive client (Prochaska et al., 1992).

CHAPTER SUMMARY/ KEY TAKEAWAYS

CEA strategies are beneficial for addictive clients in therapy.

- Experience had shown cohesion or use of force in therapy would fail.
- Compassion/Empathy is the most important leadership qualities according to research and necessary for CEA.
- PCP is client focus.
- Good planning leading to positive changes in people's lives and services is the objective of PCP.
- Client engagement approach literally involves talking, speaking, interacting, and communicating with client to build a therapeutic relationship.
- CEA & PCP when integrated capable of providing excellent services to addictive clients.
- MI enhances CEA strategies.
- MI is a PCP approach of communication of addictive stress clients.
- MI described as a goal-oriented and therapeutic approach strategy.
- MI, focus approach strategy motivation addictive clients to change and resolving ambivalence.
- MI coupled with CEA are critical in achieving desired result in therapy.
- The responsibility to change lies within the client.

The next chapter deals with evidence-based techniques used for combating effect of stress and psychological disorders of clients suffering from addiction. The techniques (e.g. CBT & PT) have stood test of time and globally accepted by clinicians and behavioral scientists.

PART II

IDENTIFYING FORMIDABLE BASED TECHNIQUES FOR THE EFFECT OF STRESS ON ADDICTION

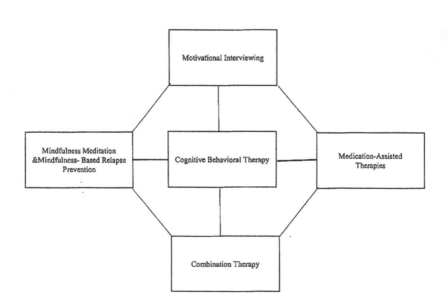

Cognitive behavioral therapy (CBT)

The impact of stress on addiction felt in the general population as technology and drug addictions are the talk of the day. The addictive stress has negatively affected health of clients, families, consumers, communities, and society. Stress can affect recovery from addictive disorders due to accessibility to drugs in American society. CBT and PT are two empirically and evidence based interventions that have demonstrated efficacy in reducing addictive stress. The integration of the two modalities were formidable effective strategies for reducing symptoms to combat the negative effects of addictive stress.

The originator of the cognitive-behavior therapy (CBT) was Dr. Aaron Beck. CBT used in treatment of psychological disorders including, but not limited to depression, anxiety, PTSD, psychosis, schizophrenia, bipolar disorder, and other psychiatric illness. It has become the most globally accepted and research evidence-based psychological intervention (Chittendan & Anthony, 2013). Beck's cognitive therapy has opened frontiers in cognitive –behavioral psychotherapy. Because of new research on psychological and addictive stress, disorders going on every day many cognitive behavioral techniques for therapy discovered and integrated with the mainstream orthodox cognitive therapy. Despite the universal cognition for CBT founded by Beck, more breakthrough in behavior technology have added cognitive- based therapies for the treatment of clients of addictive stress suffering from depression, anxiety and related psychiatric disorders (Abel, Henley, Adele & Kuyken, 2016).

Clinicians, care providers and mental health professionals should apply different forms of CBT techniques based on peculiar demands of client. Cognitive restructuring is useful for addictive stress clients who might want to commit suicide. Clients should be able to learn and recognize the dangers of killing one self and replace negative thought with positive ones. When interviewing person who wanted to commit suicide, one of the questions asked is what matters most to the client. The addictive stress client might answer in this way: "I want to take care of my children or grand kids." This positive remark about the future expectations of the suicidal person might help in preventing suicide. CBT used systematically as form of talk therapy similar to MI to change the thought process. Care providers and clinicians should practice modelling whereby accepted behavior demonstrated to clients to adhere in practice (Hallis et al, 2016).

Mindfulness training is essential where clients of addictive stress can replace negative thoughts like for example, I want kill myself with the gun. This changed by cognition, no, I cannot kill myself, no, and I do not want to die by shooting myself because it is a bad behavior with positive thought. Due to high suicide rate among addictive stress clients in the COVID-19, asking questions about suicidal thoughts, ideation and behavior has becoming benchmark in evaluating clients of addiction and other psychiatric disorders. MBCT and MBSR have been useful for stress and pain-related disorders and recurrent depressive disorders respectively (Vidrine et al, 2016). Cognitive therapy remains the rallying point for behavior technology after excelling in the empirical, objective, scientific and evidence-based standards for treatment of addictive stress clients of depression and related psychological disorders (Hallies et al, 2016).

ACCEPTANCE AND COMMITMENT THERAPY (ACT)

• • • • •

ACT was among the group of "third wave" therapies that target acceptance and mindfulness methods instead of cognitive restructuring as a focal therapeutic strategy. ACT based on the principle of avoidance regarded as a universal phenomenon while CT focuses on the philosophy of "elementary realism." ACT would enable addictive stress clients and people with psychiatric disorders pinpoints the role of thinking, feelings from emotions and sensations of addiction and why their occurrence. ACT allows relationships with cognition and flexibility in a psychological approach to addictive stress clients. This would enable clients to accept challenges from their experiences with addiction and psychological disorders and lived a value-oriented lifestyle (Hallis et al, 2016).

Recent studies have shown ACT to be useful for the treatment of depression and related mental disorders supported by evidence-based practice. Discoveries from meta-analytic studies and randomized trials have shown effectiveness of ACT in the treatment of addictive stress clients and people suffering psychiatric illness of chronic pain, depression, anxiety disorders, obstructive compulsive disorders (OCD), and psychosis just as CBT. The success rate remarkable when mindfulness combined and integrated as a therapeutic procedure between ACT and mindfulness-based cognitive therapy (MBCT). The latter adopted as an effective technique for the treatment of recurrent depression in the absence of cognitive restructuring. When cognitive restructuring was combined with MBCT based on a case study of addictive stress clients and clients of psychological disorders of recurrent depression, the recidivism rate was drastically reduced (Hallis et al, 2016).

DIALECTICAL BEHAVIOR THERAPY (DBT)

· · · · ·

The dialectical behavior therapy (DBT) introduced by Marsha Linehan was effective for the treatment of addictive stress clients with suicidal ideation, borderline personality disorder (BPD0, bulimia nervosa and related mental disorders. DBT based on the philosophical ideology of dialectics, the balancing of opposites and contrasting opinions. Linehan integrated acceptance-based therapy and mindfulness skills into DBT. DBT borne out of a desire to make a difference in the lives of addictive stress clients who are not comfortable with a traditional behavioral approach to treatment based on changing their addictive experiences.

The concept of validation was a pivot principle for therapy used in DBT. DBT integrated acceptance and mindfulness and retained tenets of cognitive-behavioral based therapies. The practice was successful in treatment of addictive stress clients with BPD. The essence of the therapy was to forge a balance and synthesize change and acceptance in behavior techniques used in therapy. DBT intervention did not apply cognitive restructuring but recognized problematic cognitive patterns as behaviors not observed (Hallies et al, 2016).

COMBINATION THERAPY

· · · · ·

The cognitive behavioral-based therapies have emerged with different applications for the treatment of addictive stress clients of depression, anxiety, schizophrenia, diabetes, pain, binge eating, suicidal behavior and other clinical disorders. Since cognitive behavior therapy was the groundwork for effective treatment for depression and other psychiatric disorders, other cognitive behavioral therapies have stepped up to support the intervention if lapses occur. When cognitive therapy (CT) combined with cognitive-behavioral based therapies such as ACT, DBT, and CBTs for the treatment of depression and related disorders, the results obtained were outstanding. The focus of CT was to change the composition of thinking, develop strategies for training people to accept and avoid painful thoughts.

CBT described as a psychotherapy with a combination of cognition (thinking) and behavioral (acting techniques). The target of CBT was to decrease or eliminate negative automatic thoughts with the purpose of changing the negative thoughts distortions and beliefs. Behavior therapy acts on symptoms by transforming environmental and behavioral factors that regulate behavior (Kinsells & Garland, 2008).

COMPASSION FOCUSED THERAPY (CFT)

• • • • •

Compassion focused therapy (CFT) was used for addictive stress clients suffering from depression, pain, and anxiety. The model noted significant fundamental processes present (e.g. shame and self-criticism) found in depression and anxiety due to addiction and psychological disorders. It relied on the social evolutionary theory of attachment and neurophysiological strategies to affect regulation. The CFT model examined the impact of compassion to raise our supporting system. This would help to balance affect-regulating systems in case of responding to the threat system. The model differentiated between treatment and therapeutic relationship and other processes included in specific training in compassion with the client. The CFT includes special training, compassion attention, cognition, behavior, and imagery, which constitutes compassion mind training (CMT). The role of compassion as an important value coveted by all care providers, mental health professionals, and clinicians cannot be over-emphasized. This used regularly as a benchmark therapy for addictive stress clients and clients of other related mental health disorders (Ashworth et al, 2015).

MEDICATION-ASSISTED THERAPIES (MATS)

• • • • •

Pharmacotherapy described as the application of medications on SUDs, addictive stress disorders, and other related psychological disorders. Currently, there has been a rise in the use of pharmacotherapy referred to as MATs. Medications such as methadione, maltrexone, and buprenorphine have been useful in reducing addictive stress due to lower costs of drugs, reduction in overdose risk, increase in social functioning and improvement in compliance to treatment (Roman, Abraham, & Knudsen, 2011). Pharmacotherapy might reduce the adverse effects of drug craving and control relapse from victims of addictive stress (Berlin, Singleton, Heishman, 2013. Moore et al, 2014).

CHAPTER SUMMARY/ KEY TAKEAWAYS

Techniques used for reducing the negative effect of stress on addiction were formidable, evidence-based interventions.

- PT & CBT are identified empirically and evidence-based interventions.
- CBT has become the most globally accepted and research evidence-based psychological interventions.
- CT rallying point for behavior technology for the treatment of addictive stress and psychological disorders (e.g. depression).
- CBT has metamorphosed into ACT, DBT & Mindfulness Interventions.
- ACT one of the "third wave" targeted acceptance and mindfulness methods.
- The concept of validation as a pivot principle used in DBT.
- The use of combination therapy based cognitive-behavioral therapies worthwhile.
- CFT based on the impact of compassion as a formidable therapy to combat addictive stress.
- Pharmacotherapy referred to as MATS essential in drug therapy of clients with addictive stress and other psychiatric illness.

In the next chapter, Positive Psychology (PT) as a new paradigm in Psychology has demonstrated efficacy in reducing the impact of addictive stress and other psychological disorders.

Establishing Positive Psychology Values (PT)

P T a new paradigm introduced by Dr. Martin Seligman, is a science that deals with positive aspects of human life and its essence to improve human flourishing and optimal functioning. The applications of PT covered all areas of human including but not limited to adolescents, adults, executives, and tribal people. The approach is useful for psychologists, clinicians, care providers and mental health professionals when dealing with various demands of the clients especially those suffering from addictive stress. This new psychology regarded as a paradigm shift from faith to evidence (Biswas-Diener, 2013).

Dr. Martin Seligman is the founder and originator of the positive psychology theory and its establishment in 1998. The pioneering work by psychologist Martin Seligman in 1998 as the then

President of the American Psychological Association (APA) observed that the dominant psychology worldview was concentrated on problem. This necessitated by the aftermath of World War II when much attention directed on the instant problems of trauma and depression and this sets the path in defining modern psychology. Thus, most research and intervention over the past 50 years of the previous century applies a unique approach of tackling the problems of anxiety, depression, schizophrenia, and suicide and drug abuse. These problems related to the impact of stress on addiction better described as addictive stress. He suggested in his presidential address to ask salient questions: "What is going right with people?' and included what is going wrong with people; and he used this professional premise to establish a new branch of science called positive psychology.

Positive theorists (Layous, Chancellor, Lyubomisky, Wang, & Doraiswamy, 2001) encourages positive interventions both directly and indirectly by allowing applications of positive emotions, positive thoughts, and positive behavior to improve well-being and decrease negative emotions. The purpose of positive psychotherapy to achieve the goal of enhancing positive emotions and decreasing negative emotions. One of the co-founders of the movement, Fredrickson (2001) contended strategies that PT therapeutic strategies based on community involvement and increased power of positive emotions of people in the community towards one another. This is the essence of the community support specialist providing excellent services for addictive stress clients in the community. PT deals with positive emotions and character traits of person in order to improve health and life quality of the people (Khazaei, Khazaei, & Ghanbati-H, 2017).

THE MAGIC POWER OF POSITIVE EMOTIONS

• • • • •

Positive emotions and capabilities considered as one of the best strategies for the prevention of psychological trauma for victims of addictive stress. Positive emotions can decrease negative emotions such as anxiety, depression, bipolar disorder, insomnia, and other psychological disorders occur because of the impact of stress on addiction (Lotfi & Akbarzadeh, 2014). Love and passion as care provider propels us to make a difference in client's lives. Positive emotion with smiling, being empathetic, treating clients with dignity and respect coupled with compassion equips us as better care providers. Positive emotion connects clinician therapeutically to a client who felt recognized and appreciated in therapy.

Positive interventions can also improve various cognitive abilities such as learning and decision-making (Brand et al, 2016). The application of positive emotion as a contributing factor for optimal health and well-being for client s of addicted stress has been the subject of investigation (Swani, 2014). Positive emotions might serve as antidote to addictive stress clients. Smiling face-to-face to client in therapy contagious to the delivery of best care. Imagine showing 'mean face' to a client! Imagine being callous in therapy to a client! You can imagine the end result- unproductive session! The power of positive emotions is magical and overwhelming making drastic changes in addictive clients and people's lives (Biswas-Diener, 2013).

Stephen N. Alapbe M.A., Psy.D.

DEVELOPING ENVIABLE QUALITY
OF CHARACTER STRENGTHS

· · · · ·

Positive emotions coupled with character strengths can improve lives of addictive stress clients and individuals with developmental disabilities and various psychological disorders. The benefits of character strengths are general to the society due to the enviable qualities of wisdom and knowledge, courage, humanity, justice, temperance and transcendence (Biswas-Diener, 20130. Knowledge acquired from character strengths used as a means of classification and development of positive traits. That supported universal capabilities for cognition, emotions, and behaviors that are beneficial to oneself and the community as well as improving positive life outcomes of addictive stress clients (Peterson & Seligman, 2004). Research done to establish the niche of character strengths, knowledge about people and enhancing positive results, well-being achievement, and leadership qualities (Park, Peterson & Seligman, 2004; Seligman, 2011).

Experience shown as a clinician and direct care worker that clients of addictive stress, psychological disorders and developmental disabilities can benefit substantially while applying enviable quality of character strengths. Care providers can build positive traits of diverse clients including courage and wisdom, vitality, love, kindness, forgiveness, and gratitude in the delivery of excellent treatment services. Most of the clients have these traits and clinicians should harness and integrate it in therapy. Mental health professionals and heath care professionals should not 'make calls" on the negative behaviors of addictive stress clients only but could transform it into positive traits for use in treatment with the possibility of promoting valued outcomes (Niemec, Shogren & Wehmeyer, 2017).

Character strengths, confined to the science of character defined as positive, trait-like abilities for cognition, emotion, and behavior change that benefit one self, others especially addictive stress and psychiatric illness clients (Niemec, 2014). Virtues regarded as core traits or characteristics valued by moral philosophers and religious thinkers throughout generation, and character strengths viewed as unique psychological processes that define these virtues (Peterson & Seligman, 2004). The use of character strengths might change perceptions about the traditional psychology worldview concentrated on problem. Addictive stress and psychological disorders clients that acquires most of these character strengths could overcome challenges while focusing on the personal emotions and personal character strengths he or she possesses. Acknowledging client character strengths and potentials improve human flourishing and optimal functioning as they confront vicissitudes of life.

CHAPTER SUMMARY/ KEY TAKEAWAYS

A new paradigm in psychology, Positive Psychology Theory introduced by Dr. Martin Seligman in 1998.

- A change in the traditional worldview of problem (negative) to positive
- PT regarded as a paradigm shift from faith to evidence.
- PT deals with positive aspects of human life and its essence to improve human flourishing and optimal functioning.
- The purpose of positive psychotherapy to achieve the goal of promoting positive emotions and reducing negative emotions.
- PT therapeutic strategies based on community involvement and increased power of positive emotions of people in the community towards one another.
- PT deals with positive emotions and character traits of person to improve health and life quality of the people.
- The benefits of character strengths are general to the society due to the enviable qualities of wisdom and knowledge, courage, humanity, justice, temperance and transcendence.
- Positive emotions & character strengths can improve lives of addictive stress clients.
- Clinicians and care providers can apply character strengths and positive emotions to make a difference in client's life.
- The use of character strengths might change perceptions about the traditional psychology worldview concentrated on problem.

In the next chapter, fundamental elements of client engagement approach used in therapy to alleviate addictive stress and psychological disorder clients discussed below.

Fundamental Elements of Client Engagement Approach

n general, engagement described as a driving force for decisions, interactions, and rooted in connections with clients ensuring active participation in therapy over time (Temkin, 2008). The groundwork of successful engagement involves healthy attachment and exchange of positive emotions towards achieving the goal of therapy (Bowlboy, 1987, 1988). Psychologically from historical perspective, Carl Rogers was one of the pioneers who emphasized the essence of engaging a client in therapy (Journal of Consulting Psychology). To sustained client's focus in therapy sessions requires continuous focus on building a strong bond, acceptance of clients without distinction, non-judgmental coupled with empathy, effective communication and listening attentively. Clinicians, and care providers can apply CEA based on choice because one concept cannot fit all requirements in therapy (Rogers, 1957).

BUILDING EXTRAORDINARY
THERAPEUTIC RELATIONSHIP

• • • • •

One of the greatest predictors of successful treatment based on research is therapeutic relationship with the clients (Knoblock-Fedders, 2008). Edward Bordin, one of the pioneers of "good therapeutic relationship" defined the concept as consisting of three essential qualities: an emotional bond of trust, caring, and respect, goals of therapy agreement, and collaboration on the "work" or tasks of the treatment. Several strategies suggested for building a strong therapeutic relationship with clients include inter alia: welcoming presence of client, awareness of time involved in therapeutic relationship, non-judgmental, emotions management, talk about what demands from therapy, asking more or different questions based on clients' needs, appreciation of client and preparatory for referral to another therapist (Hatcher, 1999).

The building an extraordinary therapeutic relationship with client might enhance successful therapy. One of the most effective element of the therapeutic relationship reiterated is building a trusting relationship with empathy, genuineness, and trust, a strong rapport cemented with ultimate goal of communicating and directing clients towards healing (Bowby, 1987, 1988). The onus on care providers and clinicians is to follow religiously inherent qualities mentioned above in practice. Clients' demands emotional bond of trust, caring and respected by care providers. Care providers should be equipped and guided by these qualities and used it efficiently in therapy. Despite your good intentions in providing excellent care for client of addictive stress, do not lost sight of the fact that your positive emotions and management matters. Clients deserve treated with respect and dignity, appreciate their efforts and commendations as well as observing their wants might lead to a productive session in therapy. Care provides should be proactive and flexible in therapy so that they do not get on their nerves in therapy.

EFFECTIVE THERAPEUTIC COMMUNICATION.

• • • • •

Effective therapeutic communication connects with building a strong therapeutic relationship. Effective therapeutic communication forms a strong alliance of trust and empathy between clients and care providers in treatment. The Medical Dictionary (2000) defined therapeutic communication as an interaction between a health care provider and a client with the goal of improving client's comfort, safety, trust and emotional/mental well-being. Effective therapeutic communication depends on building extraordinary therapeutic relationship.

The Nursing profession captures holistically essence of therapeutic communication in practice. Therapeutic communication has become a basic course for all nursing students and integrated in fundamental nursing curriculum (Porter & Porter, 2005). The importance of effective therapeutic communication regarded as an indispensable tool for health care providers and mental health professionals over-emphasized in treatment. The onus on professionals to acquire these skills and knowledge and apply it verbally and non-verbally in delivery of excellent care to addictive stress clients. Effective therapeutic communication described as a professional strategy embedded in empathy to enhance knowledge and reduce stress of addictive stress clients including caregivers. The effective utilization of this skill in therapy might serve as a win-win compromise between clients and care providers in treatment (O'Gara & Fairhust, 2004). Therapeutic communication creates a healing relationship between a client and caregiver in therapy.

THE MANTRA OF EMPATHY

. . . . .

Empathy has become a motto in the delivery of excellent services to consumers or clients. Empathy is one of the most fundamental elements of CEA and crucial as people are experiencing divers kind of addictive stress and psychological disorders (e.g. depression). Data shown by Mental Health (Qualtrics) postulates the rise in mental cases caused by COVID-19 pandemic and the ways people work and go about their lives have changed dramatically.

Qualtrics discovered from a global study reveals 42 percent of people experienced a decline of mental health. Specifically, the research discovers 67 percent have seen an elevated level of stress, 57 percent experienced increase anxiety, 54 percent emotionally exhausted, 53 percent sad, 56 percent irritable, 28 percent enhanced concentration problem, 20 percent slack to finished tracks, 15 percent cognitive problem and 12 percent challenged with juggling responsibilities.

The application of empathy as CEA contributes to positive outcomes both in business, health care services. Positive emotion in delivery of excellent care service goes hand in hand with empathy. Empathy is a powerful antidote for addictive stress client and people with psychiatric illness. A CEA based empathy should imbibe the principle of positive emotion for positive experiences in delivery of excellent service to clients. The mantra of empathy has become a pivotal work ethics for nurses, clinicians, mental health professionals, and a must generally for all care providers (Forbes, 2020-Leadership: The Power of a Client Engagement Strategy).

COMPASSION MIND TRAINING (CMT)

· · · · ·

Compassion-focused therapy (CFT) based CMT is a crucial fundamental element of client engagement approach. The CFT includes special training, compassion attention, cognition, behavior, and imagery constitutes CMT (Ashworth et al, 2015). The model described as a motivational integration and multimodal approach to working with shame and self-criticism (Gilbert, 2009, 2010, 2014), specially designed for clients suffering from addictive stress and other mental health disorders (Gilbert & Irons, 2005; Gilbert & Procter, 2006). Primarily, CFT help addictive stress clients and victims of psychiatric illness attained well-being despite difficulties experienced in mental health conditions.

CFT considered a relatively unique form of psychotherapy developed for people with mental health challenges associated with high shame and self-criticism. CFT shows promise as a worthwhile intervention for mood disorders of addictive stress clients especially high in self-criticism. Also used as intervention for various psychological disorders that includes depression, anxiety and schizophrenia (Spring & Neville, 2011). Dalai Lama (2011) defined compassion as reaction to suffering in self and others with intention to alleviate suffering and preventing it. This definition has its root in Buddha's tradition. CFT is becoming global movement using compassion as a potent force in providing benefits to various sectors especially in the healthcare sector as one of the fundamental elements in CEA and in the providing excellent service for addictive stress clients and other mental illness.

CMT is one of the significant element coveted by clinicians, mental health professionals and other care providers. CMT is a virtue of self –compassion in therapy capable of reducing distress and enhancing well-being of addictive stress clients and other psychological disorders. The onus on care providers is to train their minds and develop unique strategies based on evidence approach and intervention to deliver excellent service to the clients. Practitioners can integrate CBT and PT coupled with CMT to address various challenges of addictive stress clients and other mental illness. Addictive stress clients requires compassion attention in treatment.

Compassion intertwine empathy described the most important leadership quality according to research (Forbes, 2020-Leadership: The Power of a Client Engagement Strategy). Compassion and empathy are indispensable elements of CLEA in therapy and works together for providing excellent services to clients of various psychological disorders and addiction. Empathy as the most important leadership quality in business applies the same way to mental health professionals as a dependable strategy and element for treatment. The addictive stress clients and people suffering from psychiatric illness benefits maximally for the use of CFT. The mentioned cohorts are vulnerable to suicidal thoughts and behavior, schizophrenia, depression, paranoia, delusional, psychosis and other co-occurring disorders (e.g. bipolar). Clinicians and care providers should apply CFT based CMT for maximum result.

Most health care corporations in America adopted "Compassion" as one of their cardinal values in the delivery of excellent care to clients. The onus is on all health care providers to adopt and implement the value of compassion as a philosophy in treatment services. CFT originated by Paul Gilbert (2000) response especially for clients of psychological disorders and addictive stress who overlooked with shame and self-criticism unable to raise their voices in traditional therapy. CFT based CMT entails salient attributes to apply in therapy. Compassion feeling for one another or others, compassion feeling from others to ourselves, and compassion directed self-compassion (Gilbert, 2004). These attributes culminate to compassionate mind training (CMT) describes specifically to develop compassionate attributes and skills (Gilbert, 2009b).

KNOWLEDGE OF A-B-C ELEMENTS

• • • • •

The knowledge of antecedence (A), behavior (B) and consequence (C) elements in applied behavior analysis are crucial in CEA. Care providers, clinicians, therapists and mental health professionals confronts behavior challenged and violent clients of addiction and psychiatric illness regularly in delivery of care. The way and manner professionals reacts to the serious mental disorders of clients matters. The CEA should understand nuances of client especially challenged and violent type during behavioral assessment. The antecedence, what comes before action or behavior, what client is doing and the result or consequence should act as guiding principles in delivery of excellent care to this group of clients. Being aware of the special circumstance of addictive stress and psychiatric clients, care providers equipped the best intervention to apply based on applied behavior analysis principles (Cooper, Heron, & Heward, 2007).

ABA (Applied Behavior Analysis) principles are worthwhile in CEA for addictive stress and psychological disorders clients. The ACT as a behavior analytic approach connects CEA to tackle verbal behavior problems of addictive stress clients. The primary goal of ACT is to enhance psychological flexibility. This entails engagement with clients of addiction with the hope of living a satisfactory lifestyle. The model of psychological flexibility empowers addictive stress clients' braveness in contact with present circumstance experience despite negative thoughts and feelings (Hayes et al, 2004).

CHAPTER SUMMARY/KEY TAKEAWAYS

To get optimum result in therapy, care providers' awareness and knowledge of the fundamental elements of CEA matters.

- Engagement is a driving force for decisions, interactions, and rooted in connections with clients ensuring active participation in therapy over time is sacrosanct.
- The groundwork of successful engagement involves healthy attachment and exchange of positive emotions towards achieving the goal of therapy.
- One of the greatest predictors of successful treatment based on research is therapeutic relationship with the clients.
- Edward Bordin, one of the pioneers of "good therapeutic relationship" defined the concept as consisting of three essential qualities: an emotional bond of trust, caring, and respect, goals of therapy agreement, and collaboration on the "work" or tasks of the treatment.
- Effective therapeutic communication forms a strong alliance of trust and empathy between clients and care providers in treatment.
- The Nursing profession captures holistically essence of therapeutic communication in therapy.
- Empathy has become a motto in the delivery of excellent care to clients and a must for all care providers.
- CMT is a virtue of self-compassion in therapy.
- The knowledge of A-B-C elements crucial in CEA.

EPILOGUE/CONCLUSION

The Effect of Stress on Addiction: A Consumer Engagement Approach is must read book for mental health professionals, clinicians, nurses, therapist and the general population for the current dispensation. The effect of stress on addiction is everywhere in our daily lives in America and globally exacerbated by the COVID-19 pandemic. Addiction caused stress manifested in the food we eat, drinking, working, drug and technology we used daily. As a result, crucial steps needed to tackle this malady in our individual lives. CEA is a systematic approach used in treatment to get to the root of the matter for clients of addictive stress and mental health disorders. The integration of evidence based techniques of CBT & PT worthwhile in reducing the negative effects of addiction. Clinician and care providers need CEA strategies of MI. PCP, and empathy in combating addictive stress. The fundamental elements of therapeutic relationship and therapeutic communication, CFT/CMT, positive emotion, empathy and A-B-C elements are necessary to achieve desired outcome in therapy.

To target the best result in treatment, CBT and PT should incorporate strategies and elements of CEA. Clients expect treated with dignity and respect, compassion and love in therapy. CMT and empathy are guiding tools in CEA to build therapeutic relationship, bond of trust, and therapeutic communication in therapy.

BIBLIOGRAPHY

Acuffet al., (2018). Access to environmental reward mediates the relation between posttraumatic Stress symptoms and alcohol problems and craving. Experimental $ Clinical Pharmacology. American Psychological Association. 1-9.

Abel, S., Henley, W., Adele, M., H., & Kuyken, W. (2016). Sudden gains in Cognitive Behavioral Therapy for treatment-resistant depression. Process of Change. Journal Of Counseling & Clinical Psychology, 84(8), 726-737.

Al-Barashdi, H., S., Bouazza, As, & Jabur, N.H. (2015). Smartphone Addiction among University Undergraduates: A literature review. Journal of Scientific Research &. Reports, 4(3), 210-2015.

Alcoholics Anonymous (1953). Twelve steps and twelve traditions. New York Author.

American Psychiatric Association (2013). The Diagnostic and Statistical Manual of Mental Disorders (DSM-5).

American Psychiatric Association, 2013. Internet Gaming Disorder, Diagnostic and statistical Manual of mental disorders (5 thed.). American Psychiatric Publishing, Arlington, VA.

AshwOrth et al. (2015). An exploration of compassion focused therapy following acquired Brain injury. Psychology & Psychotherapy Theory, Research & Practice, 88, 143-162

Bergen-Cico, D, Possemato. K., & Cheon, S. (2013). Examining the efficacy of a brief Mindfulness-based stress reduction (Brief MBSR) Program on Psychological Health. Journal of American College Health, 6(6), 348-360

Biswas-Diener, R. (2013). Invitation to Positive Psychology: Research and Tools. For the Professional. Create Space Independent Publishing Platform

Block S.H., Block, C, & Peters, J. (2012). Mind-Body Workbook for stress. Effective tools For Life Stress Reduction and Crisis Management. Oakland, CA: Harbinger.

Boomvisuchi, T., & Kuladee, S. (2017). Association between Internet addiction and depression in Thai medical students at Faculty of Medicine, Ramathibodi Hospital, Plos One, 12(3), 1-10.

Brailovskaia, J., & Magraf, J. (2017). Facebook Addiction Disorder (FAD) among German, Students - longitudinal approach. Mental Health Research & Treatment Center, Germany, Bochum.12 (12), 1-15.

Chamberlain et al. (2016). Behavioral addiction-A rising tide? European. Neuropsychopharmacology, 26, 841-855.

Chen et al., (2017). Sleep disturbance and its associations with severity of dependence, Depression and quality of life among heroin-dependent patients: a cross-sectional Descriptive study. Substance Abuse Treatment, Prevention, and Policy. 1-8.

Centers for Disease Control and' Prevention (2016). Data and Statistics from Drug Overdose. http://cdc.gov/ncbddd/fasd/data.html

Chittenden, D., & Anthony, P. (2013). A cognitive behavioral approach to working parents and Families. Community Practitioner, 86(12), 1-1

Cole et al. (2012). Tobacco use and psychiatric comorbidity among adolescent's in Substance abuse treatment. Journal of Abuse Treatment, 43, 20-29.

Dean, L.D., Gress-Smith, JL., & Breitenstein, R.S. (2015). Multi-method assessments of sleep over the transition to college and the associations with depression and anxiety symptoms. *Journal of Youth and Adolescence, 44(2), 389-404.*

Dilkes-Frayne, E., Fraser, S., Pienar, K., & Kokanovic, R. (2017). Iterating "*addiction': Residential relocation and the Spatio-temporal production of alcohol and other drug consumption patterns, *Internal Journal of Drug Policy, 44: 164-173.*

Dilkes-Frayne, E. & Duff, c. (2017). Tendencies and trajectories: The production of subjectivity in an event of drug consumption. Society and Space, 35: 951--967

Doba, K. (2014). Is there a family profile of addictive behaviors? Family Functioning in Anorexia Nervosa and Drug Dependence Disorder. Journal of Clinical Psychology. (70)1), 107-117.

Dworkin, E, R., Wanklyn, S., Stasiewicz, P., R., & Coffey, S., F. (2018). PTSD symptom Presentation among people with alcohol and drug use disorders: comparison by substance Of abuse. Addictive Behaviors, (76), 188-194.

Duff, C. (2013a). The place and time of chugs. International Journal of Drug Policy, 25:633639.

Duff, C. (2013). The social life of drugs. *International Journal of Drug Policy, 24: 167-172.*

Fareed et al. (2013). Comorbid Posttraumatic Stress Disorder and Opiate Addiction: A Literature Review. *Journal of Addictive Diseases. 32 (2), 168-179*

Fortney, L., Luchterhand, C., Zakletskaia, L., Zgierska, A., & Rakel, D. (2013). Abbreviated. Mindfulness intervention for job satisfaction, quality of life, and compassion in primary care clinicians: A pilot study. Annals of Family Medicine, I I (5), 412-420.

Goeders, N. E. (2003). The impact of stress on addiction. European Neuropsychopharmacology. 15, 435-441.

Goings, T., C, Hidalgo, S., T., & McGovem, P.P. (2018). Racial/Ethnic differences in cigarette Use trends in the United States among multiracial and other youth 1994-2008. Journal of Drug Issues, 48(1), 90-105.

Guan et al. (2017). Effect of job strain and job burnout, mental fatigue, and chronic diseases Among civil servants in the Xinjiang Uygur autonomous region of China. *International Journal of Environmental Research & Public Health. 14, 872, 1-15.*

Gass, J., C, & Tiffany, S., t. (2017). Craving and Tobacco Use: Development of the choice behavior under cued conditions (CBUCC) Procedure. Psychology ofAddictive Behaviors, 1-8. Fareed et al. (2013). Comorbid Posttraumatic Stress Disorder and Opiate Addiction: A Literature Review. Journal of Addictive Diseases. 32 (2), 168-179

Gibbs et al. (2015). Cannabis use and mania symptoms: A systematic review and meta-analysis. *Journal of Affective Disorder. 171, 39-47.*

Griffiths, M. D. (2012). Internet sex addiction: a review of empirical research. Addiction Research and Theory, 20, 1 11-124.

Hallies et al. (2016). Combining cognitive behavioral therapy with acceptance & commitment Therapy for depression. A manualized group therapy, *Journal of Psychotherapy Integration, 26(2), 186-201.*

Henningfield, 1., E, Buchhalter, A., E., & Fant, R., V. (2016). Behavioral Pharmacology: Contributions to Regulation of Drug and Tobacco Products by the Food & Drug Administration. Behavior Analyses, Research & Practice, 15(4), 179-189

Hooten eta al. (2017). A conceptual framework for understanding unintended prolonged Opioid use. Mayo Foundation for Medical Education and Research. 92(12), 1822-1830.

King, D, L, Herd, M., C., E, & Delfabbro, Fl., P. (2018). Motivational components of tolerance in Internet gaming disorder. Computers in Human Behavior, 78, 133-141.

King, D.L., Kaptsis, D, Delfabbro, P. H., & Gradisar, M. (2017). Effectiveness of brief abstinence for modifying problematic Internet gaming cognitions and behaviors. Journal of Clinical Psychology.

King, D. L., Madeleine, C, E., H., & Delfabbro, P., H. (2018). Motivational component tolerance in Internet gaming disorder. Computers in Human Behavior, 78: 133-141.

King, D.L., Kaptsisd. Delfabbro, P.H., & Gradisar, M. (2017). Effectiveness of brief Abstinence for modifying problematic Internet gaming cognition and behaviors. Journal of Clinical Psychology.

Kress et al., (2018). The use of relational-cultural theory in counseling clients who have traumatic stress disorders. Journal of Counseling & Development, 96(1), I -12.

Khazaei, F., Khazaei, 0., & Ghanbari-H, B. (2017). Positive psychology interventions for Internet addiction treatment. Computers in Human Behavior, 72, 314-31 1.

Kuss et al. (2018). Problematic mobile phone use and addiction across generations: the roles of psychopathological symptoms and smartphone use. Journal of Technology in Behavioral Science, 1-5.

Kuss, D.L., & Grffiths, MD. (2012). Internet gaming addiction: A systematic review of empirical research. International Journal of Mental Health and Addiction, 10(2), 278-309.

Kuss, J.D, & Lopez-Femandez, O. (2016). Internet addiction and problematic Internet use. A Systematic review of clinical research. World Journal of Psyhiatry,6(1), 143-176.

Lang, B., & Rosenberg, H. (2017). Public Perceptions of Behavioral & Substance Addictions. Psychology of Addictions Behavior, 1 1(1), 79-84

Lomas, T. (2016). Second Wave Positive Psychology: Exploring the positive-negative dialectics of wellbeing. Journal of Happiness Studies, 1753-1768. review and meta-analysis protocols (PRISMA-P) 2015 statement.

Mumba, M., N, Findlay, L., J., & snow, D, E. (2018). Treatment Options for opioid Use Disorders: A Review of the Relevant Literature, 29(3), 221-22

Niemiec, R., M., Shogren, K., A., & Wehmeyer, M., L. (2017). Character Strengths and Intellectual and Developmental Disability: A Strengths-Based Approach from Positive Psychology. Education and Training in Autism and Developmental Disabilities, 52(1), 13-25.

Mumba, M., N, Findlay, L., J., & snow, D, E. (2018). Treatment Options for opioid Use Disorders: A Review of the Relevant Literature, 29(3), 221-22. Developmental Psychology, 5 1 (2), 248-259.

Otto et al. (2017). Genetic Variation in the Exome: Associations with Alcohol & Tobacco Co-use. Psychology of Addictive Behaviors, 1-13.

Ousda et al. (2018). The impact of traumatic stress on Pavlovian biases. Psychological Medicine, 48, 327-336. Autism and Developmental Disabilities, 52(1), 13-2

Paulson, S., Davidson, R., Jha, A., & Kabat-Zinn, J. (2013). Becoming conscious: The science of mindfulness. Annals of the New York Academy of Sciences, 1303, 87-104

Peterson, C, & Seligman, M.E.P. (2004). Character strengths and virtues: A handbook and classification. New York: Oxford.

Pontes, H. M., Kiraly, O., Demetrovics, Z, & Griffiths, M.D. (2014). The conceptualization and measurement of DSM-5 internet gaming Disorder: The development of the 1CD-20 test.

Ren, Y., Yang, L, & Liu, L. (2017. Social Anxiety and Internet Addiction among rural left- behind children: the mediating effect of loneliness. 46(12), 1659-1668.

Richardson, T., H. (2013). Substance misuse in depression and bipolar disorder: a review of psychological interventions and consideration.

Ren, Y., Yang, L, & Liu, L. (2017. Social Anxiety and Internet Addiction among rural left- behind children: the mediating effect of loneliness. 46 (12), 1659-1668.

Richardson, T., H. (2013). Substance misuse in depression and bipolar disorder: a review of psychological interventions and considerations for clinical practice. Ment. Health Subst. Use 6, 76-93.

Rosen, D, Hunsaker, As, Cornelius, J., R., & Reynolds, C, F. (2011). Characteristics and consequences of heroin use among older adults in the United States: a review of the literature, treatment implications, and recommendations for further research. 36(4), 279-285.

Sharma, P., Bharati, A, De Sousa, A., & Shah, N. (2016). Internet Addiction and its association with psychopathology: A study in schoolchildren from Mumbai, India. Journal of Community ofMedicine, 7(1), 1-4.

Snodgrass et al. (2018). The partial truths of compensatory and poor-get-poorer internet use theories: more highly involved videogame players experience greater psychosocial benefits. Computers in Human BEHAVIOR, 78,10-25.

Shu, C., & Cook, B., L. (2015). Examining the association between substance use disorder & smoking cessation. Society for the Study of Addiction. 1016-1024.

Simpson, T.L., Stappenbeck, C.A., Laurek, JA., JA., Lehavor, K., & Kayren, L.D. (2014). Drinking motives moderate daily relationships between PSTD symptoms and alcohol use. Journal ofAbnormal Psychology, 123, 237-247.

Smith, K.Z. medical opioid use and abuse and PTSD diagnosis: Interactions with sex and associations with symptom clusters. Addictive Behavior. 58, 167-174.

Smith, P.H., Cercone, S.A., medical opioid use and abuse and PTSD diagnosis: Interactions with sex and associations with symptom clusters. Addictive Behavior. 58, 167-174. e 6, 76-93.

McKee, S.A., & Homish, G.G. (2016 medical opioid use and abuse and PTSD diagnosis: Interactions with sex and associations with symptom clusters. Ad Swani, P. (2014). Positive emotions: Facilitator of optimal health and wellbeing. Indian Journal of Heal[th] and Wellbeing, 5(2), 1517-151

Tavernier, R., & Willoughby, T. (2014). Sleep problems: predictor or outcome of media use among emerging Swani, P. (2014). Positive emotions: Facilitator of optimal health and wellbeing. Indian Journal Of Heal[th] and Wellbeing, 5(2), 1517-151

Thege et al. (2017). Relationship between interpersonal trauma exposure and addictive behaviors: a systematic review.

Turel, O; Brewers, D; & Bechara, S. (2018). Time distortion when users at- risk for social media Addiction engage in non-social media tasks. I-17.

Van Wormer, K., & Davis, D, R. (2016). Addiction Treatment: a strength perspective (6[th]ed). Belmont, CA. Brooks/ Cole Cengage Learning.

Vidrine et al. (2016). Efficacy of Mindfulness-based Addiction Treatment (MBAT) for Smoking Cessation and Lapse Recovery: A Randomized Clinic Trial. Journal of Counseling & Clinical Psychology, 84(9), 824-838.

Swani, P. (2014). Positive emotions: Facilitator of optimal health and wellbeing. Indian Journal Of Hea1th and Wellbeing, 5(2), 1517-151

Thege et al. (2017). Relationship between interpersonal trauma exposure and addictive behaviors: a systematic review.

Turel, O; Brewers, D; & Bechara, S. (2018). Time distortion when users at- risk for social media Addiction engage in non-social media tasks. I-17.

Van Wormer, K., & Davis, D, R. (2016). Addiction Treatment: a strength perspective (6[th]ed). Belmont, CA. Brooks/ Cole Cengage Learning.

Vidrine et al. (2016). Efficacy of Mindfulness-based Addiction Treatment (MBAT) for Smoking Cessation and Lapse Recovery: A Randomized Clinic Trial. Journal of Counseling & Clinical Psychology, 84(9), 824-838.

Vogel, E.A., Rose, J.P., Roberts, I.R., & Eckies, K. (2014). Social comparison, social media, and self-esteem. Psychology of Popular Media Culture, 3(4), 206-222.

Woods, H., C, & Scott, H. (2016). #Sleepyness: social media use in adolescence is associated with poor sleep quality, anxiety, depression and low self-esteem. Journal of Adolescence. 51, 41-49.

Zivnuska, S., Carlson, JR., Carlson, D, S., Harris, R., B., & Han-is, IQ, J. (2019). Social media addiction and social media reactions: The implications for job performance. The Journal of Social Psychology, 1-15.

ACKNOWLEDGEMENTS

The journey towards the writing of the book was not an easy one. Foremost, I thank God for His mercies, grace, wisdom and knowledge in completing the task of writing the book. I acknowledged the invaluable supervision by Dr. Linda Salvucci (PHD, Clinical Psychology) of the California Southern University during research on doctoral project: "The Impact of Stress on Addiction." The research opens horizon of various types of additions (e.g. drug and technology) plaguing the American society. Worthy to mention is Dr. Anthony Adamgbo (PHD, Organizational Development-OD) a Rebranding Expert who collaborated to create a suitable title for this book as well as proof reading, critique, making corrections and offering useful suggestions for the take-off and conclusion of the book.. Sirayira Alapbe, a final year student of Arts and Design, Lindenwood University, St. Louis, MO also helped in formatting and checking grammatical errors.

Finally, I am indebted to the services of the Saint Louis Public Library and staff of the Webster University Library for their assistance. Most of the time, I used the Berea Temple International Church of the Assembly of God for study and developing materials in writing for the book for which I am grateful to the Board.

ABOUT THE AUTHOR

D r. Stephen N. Alapbe graduated Doctor of Psychology Clinical Psychology (Psy.D, magna cum laude) from the California Southern University, Costa Mesa, California. The author also graduated from The Chicago School of Professional Psychology, Chicago with a master's degree in Psychology concentration Gerontology and a Certification ABA. The author had a Bachelor of Arts Psychology, Webster University St. Louis, MO. The author is a clinician/case manager at one of the behavioral health hospitals, St. Louis, MO. The author's research on "The Impact of Stress on Addiction" serves as a groundwork in writing the book. The author worked in different clinical settings as a psychiatric technician/therapist, habilitation specialist, direct care worker, caseworker, behavior support professional, clinician, and case manager. The experiences gained as a health care provider and clinician worthwhile and interactions with diverse client motivated passion of writing this book. The author impressed by Dr. Linda Salvucci, clinical instructor at California Southern University on the teaching of the course "The Psychology of Stress" motivated interest on doctoral research of addiction and eventually the writing of this book.

The author is a member of the APA; resides in St. Louis, MO and happily married with three children. The author is a devoted Christian, and love serving God and humanity.

Printed in the USA
CPSIA information can be obtained
at www.ICGtesting.com
LVHW040614290124
769814LV00055B/1305

9 781961 532489